Enjoy! Hope this book helps.

Mizz Liz

Other books by Elizabeth G. Honaker:

Come Before Winter (October 1, 2014)

Mizz Liz's Five Steps to Good Writing

by Elizabeth G. Honaker

Bread of Life Books

Sparta, TN

Copyright © 2014 Elizabeth G. Honaker

All rights reserved. No part of this book may be used or reproduced by any means, graphic, electronic, or mechanical, including photocopying, recording, taping or by any information storage retrieval system without the written permission of the publisher except in the case of brief quotations embodied in critical articles and reviews.

Bread of Life Books may be ordered through Amazon.com or by contacting:

Bread of Life Books
P.O. 373
Sparta, TN 38583
www.bolb.org

Cover image from Shutterstock. © Ellen Mol

ISBN-13: 978 - 1500867225
ISBN-10: 1500867225

Printed in the United States of America.

To Allen,

James & Erin & Josie,

Christine & Michael & Austin & Garrett & Dylan

Table of Contents

Introduction	ix
Step 1: Free Writing = creative juices, graphophiles, writing, bullets..................	1
Step 2: Thesis = overall idea, single sentence, noun / verb, subtle opinion............	10
Step 3: Outline = topics, Roman numerals, supporting details...........................	16
Step 4: Composition = structure, the paragraph, FPE, introductory ¶ / body / concluding ¶.............................	24
Step 5: Revision = CS vs. hack, improvement checklist, land of "good enough"...	37
Postscript 1: Types of Compositions = All kinds of definitions...........................	41
Postscript 2: A Few Suggested Exercises	43
Postscript 3: Vocabulary and Other Language Tools	45
Postscript 4: Word Processing Software	46
Farewell	51

Introduction

If there's one thing this world has plenty of, it's guides to good writing. I have read and taught out of many of them. And I do not claim to be unique in my understanding of how to write well. However, this book is a little different from other workbooks: I have created this so that I can use it *with* my students. I really, really do not believe that anyone can learn a skill like writing just from reading about it in a book, any more than I believe a person can learn to play a musical instrument just from a set of pictures, or even a DVD. These things are helpful, and I have certainly employed them throughout my teaching career, but they are not enough.

The important ingredient in teaching writing is, in my opinion, the judgment and experience of the teacher or professor. And so you, the student, will not be on your own. You will have this guide and you will have *me*. So that you can communicate with me over anything in this manual, please note my email address below:

mizzlizwriting@gmail.com

If you are my registered student, be assured that I will usually respond to your email within 24 hours (unless the internet goes crazy or the power goes out, which happens in rural Tennessee). If you have purchased my book through Amazon.com, please allow me a little more time.

You will notice that I have written 5 steps and 4 postscripts. (A postscript used to be a piece of information that one attached to a letter after one had signed his or her name. Now it is a fancy name for a certain type of computer software.) The 5 steps are simple, time-tested instructions for any writer who feels that he or she may have missed something on the first go-around; they are especially useful for younger students who have a tough time just getting started on a writing assignment or composition. The 4 postscripts are important categories of information that I usually append to my college classes in some form or another.

I am a bit of a rebel at heart: I intensely dislike (one might say *hate*) our PC world where all women are "Ms. So-and-so." So that there is no misunderstanding, my *nom de plume* is based on the good-ol' Southern habit (learned in my teenage years from my dear Aunt Terry) of calling older women "Miss Susan" or "Miss Jane" out of respect and endearment. I have been "Miss Liz" to hundreds of piano students, VBS attendees, and even students in public schools. However, my rebel side has emerged now that I am the wise side of 60, and I hereby take the liberty of spelling "Miss" as "Mizz" – the only ungrammatical dalliance I will allow in this book!

This type of manual is a new venture for me, even though I have been a writer since I was five when I wrote my first book about a girl and her horse. I have to give credit to my mother for that first book, however, because I wasn't quite up to spelling all the words on my own. I dictated, Mommie wrote, and I did all of the illustrations. Quite a printer's daughter, I was! Since then, I have been encouraged to write by many different teachers, students, and – of course – my beloved husband and best friend (we are in our 44th year of marriage as I write this).

You will notice that there are illustrations and different fonts throughout the book. My intention in all this is to engage the student writer in a new way – to help him or her get interested, even excited, about an activity that has brought me endless joy throughout my life. I hope this aspect will prove an engaging aspect of this book and not a distraction.

I envision this as a skeleton upon which students of various ages can hang their own understandings of how to communicate using the written word. I will be happy if you report success, and I plan to revise this manual if there are problems. Please let me know in either case.

In His service,

Liz Honaker

Step 1: Free writing.

> *Why do so many people dread writing?*
>
> *Why do so many students put off their writing assignments?*
>
> *One answer I get all the time is this: "I don't know how or what to write."*

Well, those days are over. We are going to write, and we are going to write TOGETHER.

The first thing we have to do is unlock our creative juices. Just like a runner does stretches, and a gymnast does warm-ups, we are going to warm up our brains and get writing right away.

Got a piece of paper and a pen? No? Well, go find a nice smooth piece of paper – nothing scratchy – and fetch yourself a pen that writes like a dream.

OK, dreamy pens – what's this all about? Well, just do what I say. Do you like ballpoints? Markers? Gel pens? Anything – any color – any size. Just grab one and find that piece of paper. Personally, I love the feel of writing with ballpoint on newspaper – but newspaper rarely has spare space on it, and you usually have to write in the margins or under headlines. That's OK. I give you permission to do that. Scribble away.

So choose your instruments and find a firm surface on which to write.

Now, before you get all worried that you are taking one step backwards in this technological age, let me reassure you. I am not a technophobe who hates computers (well, I hate *certain* computers, but let's leave that *alone* for a moment!).We will use a computer (if you have one) in a minute.

I am trying to get you to see that writing is *fun*, and it's actually a creative outlet that a student like you does not have to dread.

This breakthrough will take some time, so please just trust me right this minute and do what I say.

Got the pen and paper? Good. Now write something – one or two words – about the following topic:

SOMEONE YOU KNOW.

Write it in this book if you like.

Please don't panic at this stage. Don't think I'm crazy, because I'm not.

I'm a

graphophile

(Yes, I made that up – Microsoft doesn't even like it because there are red squiggly lines under the word as I type this. Oh, well!)

`Grapho` is Greek for "writing"; `phile` is Greek for "love". I love writing – want to join me?

Then write something down about someone you know…

Like your mother.

Or your best friend.

Or your best enemy.

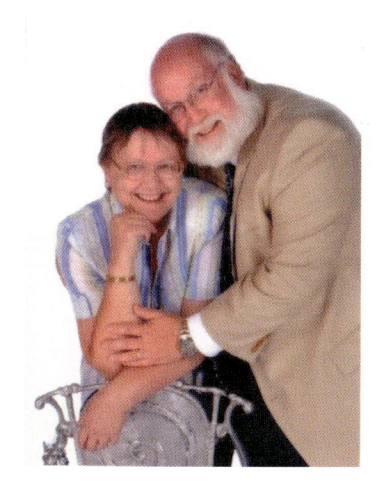

Or even this crazy professor.

I'm waiting….

Don't worry about spelling
    …or grammar
    …or sentences -- just yet !

OK, let's say that you have done what I said. You have taken your pen / marker / gel-whatever and written a word or two on the newspaper about our topic. Let's say you have chosen to write about this crazy professor. You've written the word:

Crazy

Not very imaginative, but at least you've put pen to paper (an old-fashioned saying, but it still works, doesn't it?).

Now put another word down:

Female   * * * * * * * * *

Keep going.

............................*Older woman*

Oh, WOW! You actually wrote TWO words!!! Keep going!

- - - - *Graphophile* - - - - -

Good. We have four points, which I am going to call "bullets." We need four more to go on to the next step. Can you come up with them on your own? Sure you can!! Use your best handwriting for this.

Bullet # 5: _____

Bullet # 6: _____

Bullet # 7: _____

Bullet # 8: _____

Try to write the bullets all on one side of the paper or newspaper, so we can collect them all in a minute or two. And now write an opinion about your work so far. It could read something like this:

I feel dorky doing this.

I forgot what writing with a pen feels like.

I wish we could get to the next step before I fall asleep.

Hey – maybe Mizz Liz is onto something here!

What to do next:

Using either a separate sheet of paper (this time, make it lined paper, please) or a computer, organize all the bullets like this:

Step 1: Free write on This Crazy Professor

- **Crazy**
- **Female**
- **Older woman**
- **Graphophile**
- _____
- _____
- _____
- _____

You don't have to capitalize every word – Microsoft is doing that for me automatically while I type this. In fact, don't worry about spelling or grammar at this stage – but it would sure cheer up your former English teachers to know that you remember SOME of what they've taught you!

Are you ready to go to Step 2? Well, we're almost there! Just a few more things to think about – that's right, it's time to use your noodle and organize yourself for the next step.

Assuming that you've written in the last four bullets as I've instructed you to do, you should start to see one – or maybe two – ideas emerge that are most important to you about this subject. You might like to think of it as a *pattern* – a *theme*.

Let's say that I filled in this entire free write myself, and I included the words "fun," "knowledgeable," "energetic," and "helpful" in the blanks. (Well, after all, I *have* lived with myself for quite some time now!) Do you see that these words – all except for "crazy" – seem to describe my personality or my physical appearance? So could this reveal a pattern or a theme?

Now let's go on to Step 2.

Step 2: Thesis

What one thing do you hear all the time from people who are listening to a story?

How about this: "What's the <u>point</u>?"

(Yes, a lot of students ask me that during class!)

Well, believe it or not, one of the most important things to do when you are writing more than one sentence is to tell your reader the *point* you are trying to make. That's right – you need to tell your readers where you're **going** with your composition.

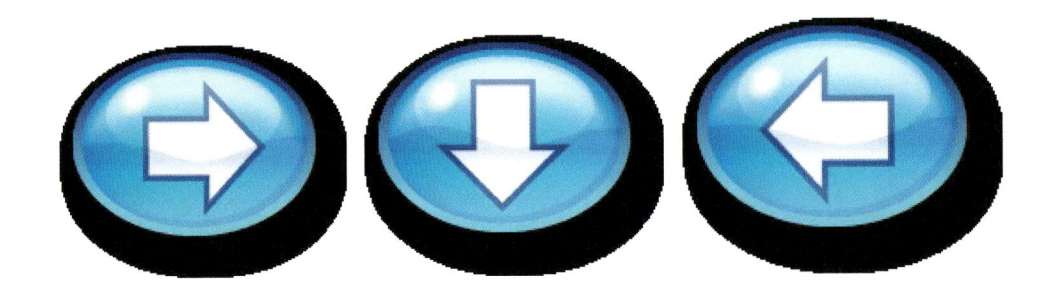

This attempt to tell your reader what your composition is all about is called a **thesis**. It is one sentence, preferably at the beginning of your first paragraph (some college professors say at the end), that gives the direction of your entire composition.

Now, at this point, you might be asking yourself, "How can I sum up the entire composition in one sentence? If I could do that, I wouldn't have to write this silly composition or essay or paper!"

The answer to this question is this:

The thesis just gives your reader the *overall idea* of your composition, not its supporting details.

Just like the frame of a house is not the *complete* house – but it is a really, really important thing to put up first – the THESIS shows where the composition is going. It gives your reader an idea of the shape and size and flavor of your paper.

And that has got to be a VERY good thing!

So let's get started on this thesis. What do we do first? One thing is to start paying attention to our grammar and spelling and rules of punctuation. From this point forward, do your best on these.

At this point, we have to talk about sentences. What is a sentence?

A sentence is a group of English words that have at least three characteristics. Let's look at them now:

Complete Idea + Two Parts + Makes sense

1. The words in a sentence express a complete idea.

Joe waters the plants.

You get a complete idea from the words. You are not expected to guess what is going on.

2. A sentence has both a subject (usually a *noun*) and an action word (a *verb*).

Joe waters the plants.

Someone ("Joe") is doing something ("waters").

3. A sentence makes sense to the reader.

Since you speak English, you know that "Joe" is someone's name. You also are familiar with what it means to "water" something. Next, you recognize "the" – which tells you that a noun is coming right after. And by now you have seen a "plant." So you can make a picture in your mind about what is happening in the sentence. Here we speak of "vocabulary" and "grammar." More on those things in Postscript 3.

Do these things sound hard or easy? The answer I want to hear from you is "easy" – because it really *is* easy!

Now, before I get started showing you how easy thesis-writing really is, I want to stress that you have to know what a NOUN and a VERB are. If you are uncertain about these two parts of speech, let's review a bit before you go on.

A noun is the name of a person, place, or thing.

Examples of common nouns: dog, chair, book, paper, building

Examples of proper nouns: Mizz Liz, Samantha, George, Sparta

When a sentence is all about a particular noun, that noun is the subject of the sentence.

Example: In the sentence "The sun shines," the *sun* is not only a noun (the only one in the sentence). It is also what the sentence is all *about*.

A verb is an action word.

What is the sun doing? It *shines*. "Shining" is an action.

And that's all there is to it.

No mystery, just some history.

Now let's walk through the process of writing a thesis on our topic about the "crazy professor" (me!).

For this part, I suggest you switch to a computer if you have one. Typing out your thesis on a computer, using word processing software (see Postscript 4 for some suggestions), will make Steps 3, 4, and 5 easier. (Did you notice I keep using that word "easy"?)

(By the way, I *am* married to Santa Claus – no joke! – and he is my computer technician.)

In order to have a good <u>thesis</u>, you have to have two more things:

1. **You have to have a sentence that gives a <u>subtle opinion</u>.**

2. **It has to be a sentence that gives an overall idea of what you are going to write about. In other words, your sentence has to be a snapshot of your entire composition, not just a part of it.**

First, what kind of sentences can we construct from our free write? Let me give you some examples:

<u>Sentence # 1</u>: *Professor Honaker is crazy.*

[This sentence is an *opinion*. "Professor Honaker" is the **subject**; "is" is the **verb**.]

<u>Sentence # 2</u>: *Mizz Liz is an older woman.*

[This sentence states a *fact*. "Mizz Liz" is the **subject**; "is" is the **verb**.]

Sentence # 3: *My writing professor is a self-proclaimed graphophile who loves to help other people become graphophiles like she is.*

[This sentence is a bit more complicated, but essentially it is an opinion expressed by the writer. The **subject** is "professor" and the **verb** is "is." All the other words add to the core idea "professor is."]

Would any of these sentences serve as a good thesis? Let's see.

Sentence #1 has an opinion, but it is not a _subtle_ opinion. (The word "crazy" is never going to be _subtle_.) Besides, where would you go with your composition once you have stated that you believe I am crazy? Repeating your belief that I am crazy ten times is not really a good composition (at least, there's no reason to say it more than once!).

Sentence # 2 is just a statement of fact; it has no opinion at all. It cannot serve as your thesis.

Sentence # 3 does contain a _subtle_ opinion, and you have a solid basis for writing a good composition about your writing professor (me!). You can talk about what a graphophile is, what I do in the classroom because I am a graphophile, and how becoming a graphophile can help you write better – and so on. Get the picture?

So let's say that Sentence # 3 will be your temporary thesis for a minute or two. (You do not have to adopt this sentence as your thesis – I'm just using this as an example.)

If you understand Steps 1 & 2, you've got your ticket to Step 3!

Step 3: Outline

It's not hard to understand that once you have a sentence that pretty much sums up the whole point of your composition, you then have to *elaborate* – you have to break down the whole thesis into **topics**.

English teachers freely use the word "topic" all the time; they talk about *topics* for papers and *topics* for research and *topics* for a paragraph. This can lead to confusion when I start talking about using *topics* to develop your thesis.

*So let's define a **topic** as one part of the explanation of your thesis. Writing which has a purpose has to have a main idea – a* thesis *– and ways to develop that idea – the* topics *.*

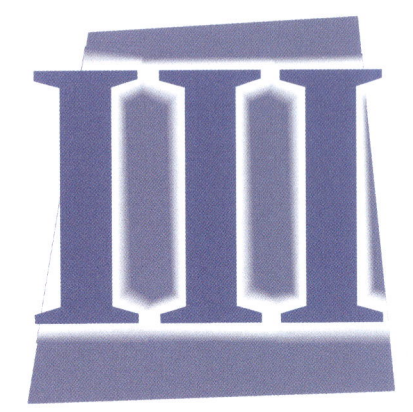

It's a good idea to use three topics to develop a thesis. A clever writer can use two, but I don't recommend that a beginner start out that way. A TERM PAPER (more than five paragraphs) will either use three topics with lots of supporting details, or use four or maybe five topics. But since we're just starting out, we're going to use three.

Let's look back at our free write. Here's where it really becomes useful. Remember those eight ideas, those eight bullets? Let's examine the ones that I contributed at first: **crazy** – **female** – **older woman** – **graphophile**. Does anything in this group suggest an explanation (in other words, some topics) of our thesis?

At first glance, nothing seems to go with **graphophile**. I could say I'm crazy over words or crazy over teaching. It would mean that I was bouncing off of the single word "crazy" and linking it with another word. That's OK to do, because as I stressed before, the free write exists to get your creative juices flowing; it's not some sort of prison where the words are locked into a certain phrase or sentence.

However, let's look at the last four words that I suggested: **fun** – **knowledgeable** – **energetic** – **helpful**. Can we link any of these to the idea of **graphophile**?

Of course we can!

Let's work with these words by starting an outline. Remember our thesis?

My writing professor is a self-proclaimed graphophile who loves to help other people become graphophiles like she is.

How can we develop this main idea? Here are some suggestions:

1. She is very knowledgeable about how a student can improve his or her writing.
2. She puts a great deal of energy into teaching each class.
3. She is one of the most helpful professors I have ever encountered in college.

I know what you're thinking at this point: She sure sounds overly confident! Well, maybe, but let's just go with these thoughts for a moment.

An outline has a special form. For the main ideas that I mentioned above, we are going to use Roman numerals, so our outline looks like this:

OUTLINE
- I. She is very knowledgeable about how a student can improve his or her writing.
- II. She puts a great deal of energy into teaching each class.
- III. She is one of the most helpful professors I have ever encountered in college.

If you think this looks a little thin, you're absolutely right. We're not finished with this outline, because this represents just the topics, not the supporting details.

Look back and see what a topic is. It is one part of developing a thesis. But it is not a single statement; it needs to be supplemented by supporting details. Let's use the first sentence in my outline (Roman Numeral I) to explain what comes next:

She is very knowledgeable about how a student can improve his or her writing.

Can we find *examples* to prove this statement? In other words, can we provide details to support this sentence? Well – since I am the professor mentioned in this sentence – I certainly can! Here goes:

- I. She is very knowledgeable about how a student can improve his or her writing and become a graphophile.
   - A. Mizz Liz gives lectures which clearly explain each step in writing.
   - B. She also gives meaningful assignments which demonstrate how to use each of the five steps.
   - C. When she grades assignments, she gives important information about where corrections can be made.

Please notice that each detail is set off by a **capital letter**, NOT a Roman numeral or ordinary number.

18

Did you notice anything about these supporting details?

- ❖ Each sentence under Roman Numeral I is based on a **fact** – something that you can check for yourself. Now, I know some people might think that the words "clearly" or "important" are opinions, but let me emphasize right now that you can <u>perceive</u> or <u>experience</u> these things and make your own <u>judgment</u>. That's important to remember.

- ❖ Each supporting detail is written in a complete sentence. Lots and lots of teachers allow students to put down a single word (or even a short phrase) into outlines. This is a bad thing, because when it comes to using the outline in Step 4 (the composition itself), the student often forgets exactly what that one word meant to him or her when he or she first wrote it.

Let me give you an example of my second bullet. Suppose for point "A" I had written one word. Let's suppose that one word was "==lectures==." You would agree with me that this word is a key word in the sentence that I gave in "A" – correct?

But let's also assume that once I had written that one word, I had walked away and had gone into the kitchen for some comfort food (a necessary part of this process, by the way – but not necessarily at this <u>exact</u> moment in time). Let's say I had eaten some raisins and had drunk a small glass of milk, and had then gone back to my writing. Could I say with 100% confidence that I would remember exactly what "lectures" meant in my outline?

I mean no disrespect to all you young whippersnappers out there, but I say this to you: In nine out of ten instances, you will _think_ you remember the connection between "lectures" and being a graphophile, but you _won't_.

Time and time again, I have seen instances where the student's original thought gets changed into something the student did not mean the first time – precisely because the student did not follow directions. Look at some examples of this:

Mizz Liz gives lectures all the time.

My professor's lectures come at the beginning of the class.

Professor Honaker uses a mixture of PowerPoint and SmartBoard technology to deliver her lectures.

(Did you notice that the picture of the lecturing professor is _backwards_? Why do you think this is so? Could it be because the above sentences are backwards?)

I've even seen something like this:

Mizz Liz's lectures are boring.

I can't understand why anyone would say this! How do they know if they're not paying attention?

Do you see that each of these alternative sentences do NOT connect to the thesis we've chosen?

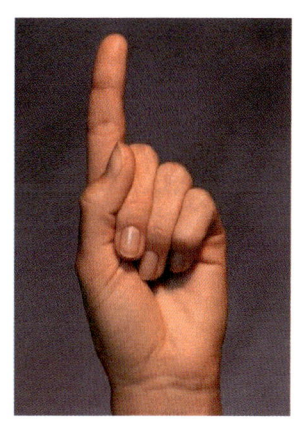

Mizz Liz gives lectures all the time.

So what? How does this prove or demonstrate I know how to turn a student into a graphophile? It doesn't. It only demonstrates that I might be a "windbag."

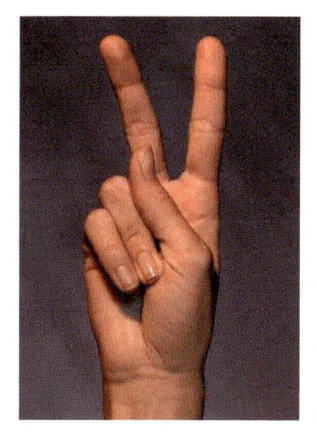

My professor's lectures come at the beginning of the class.

This may be a true statement, but how does it link to your professor – me – being a graphophile? It doesn't. It only demonstrates that I like to do things in a certain order.

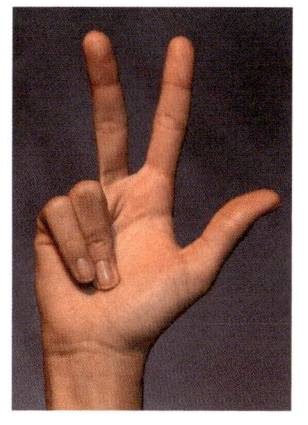

Professor Honaker uses a mixture of PowerPoint and SmartBoard technology to deliver her lectures.

Good for me! But, again – how does this support the main idea that I am a graphophile? It doesn't. It just shows the reader that I use technology in the classroom.

If you read each sentence in the *original* development of Roman Numeral I on page 18 carefully, you will soon see that each point supports the idea that I'm a graphophile who wants to help others become graphophiles.

In point "A," I want my reader to make the connection between being a *graphophile* and developing *writing skills*.

In point "B," I want my reader to make the connection between being a *graphophile* and engaging in regular *writing practice*.

In point "C," I want my reader to make the connection between being a *graphophile* and making *corrections to your writing* when needed.

At this point, I want to make it very clear that this is only one way to develop the thesis about this topic. There can be other ways, and you can do this at a later time if you wish. But let's agree that so far, so good – you at least have a good ==thesis== and good ==main topics== that make good connections to the thesis.

We need to work on the supporting details for Roman Numerals II and III before we move on to the next step.

Here's my Roman Numeral II:

    II.   She puts a great deal of energy into teaching each class.

Of course, we need examples for this topic, and since you're new to my style of teaching, I will supply you with three:

    II.   She puts a great deal of energy into teaching each class.
        A. She takes the time to prepare handouts that supplement her lectures.
        B. She constantly walks through the class during "seminar time," assisting the students in whatever ways she can.
        C. She interacts with the class like a coach would interact with a sports team.

After having examined the supporting detail from Roman Numeral I, I hope you can see that the "A," "B," and "C" under Roman Numeral II all connect with the idea of "teaching energetically." Let's tackle Roman Numeral III:

> III. She is one of the most helpful professors I have ever encountered in college.

Suppose we add *two* supporting details to this point.

Suppose we say:

A. Mizz Liz goes out of her way to encourage frightened or depressed students.

B. She is not afraid to tell you that your writing needs improvement, but she never does it to put you down.

Have we said all that we can possibly say about our thesis? Maybe. Maybe not.

The exciting thing is that we are close to working on Step 4 (Composition). There are only a few more things to say about our work so far:

- ❖ The first three steps in writing are not separate exercises. The free write, the thesis, and the outline are all supposed to work together. Be sure to keep your thesis and your outline *unified*.
- ❖ However, even at this point, nothing is "written in stone." If something in the outline does not quite fit with the thesis, go back and work at it again.
- ❖ If you change your mind about the thesis, go back and fix it, and then work on the outline to support your new thesis.

Step 4: Composition

We've arrived!! We are ready to write...

Except...we've been writing all this time – right?

So what do we do? Do we just start in and write anything that comes into our heads?

Now, that really WOULD be silly, wouldn't it? This step is supposed to build on the other three steps. It is not independent of them.

Here's good news: You've done a lot of the "hard" work already. In fact, I would say you're about to do something "**easy**"! (There's that word again!)

We're going to use another important word here: STRUCTURE.

It shouldn't frighten you. "**Structure**" is a good word. We have structure all around us every day. We live in houses that have structure. We drive on roads (that is, if you're old enough to drive!) on roads that have structure. Our day has structure – a schedule perhaps. (At the very least, you're supposed to get to class on time!)

Our bodies have structure; we have skeletons to support skin and organs and everything else.

So far, we have built structure into our writing. In **Step 1**, we started the creative juices flowing. We searched for a main idea (our thesis) for our writing in **Step 2**. In **Step 3**, we decided what topics to use to develop our thesis.

Now we're going to talk about one more type of structure, and then get started on our composition.

There is a certain form that we use when putting a basic composition together. It is called the **"Five-Paragraph Essay"** (**FPE**).

OK, up to now, I have totally ignored paragraphs. I admit it, but it's not because they are not important. We have been setting ourselves up for paragraphs, and now we will start talking about them.

A **paragraph** is a set of sentences that focuses on a single topic.

Ah-HA! We've used that word "topic" again!

For our purposes here, I will state that a paragraph has **3 – 5 sentences**. Other teachers might say something else. But let's just stick with my definition for the moment.

Since we've already tackled what a sentence is, it won't be much harder to imagine three, four, or five sentences together, all explaining one idea. So let's mention one more thing. A paragraph has to signal to the reader that it's a paragraph. We do this by indenting the first line of the group of sentences.

(If you are typing your composition on a computer, you will hit the "tab" key, which equals 5 spaces. Do not type in five individual spaces; it sometimes causes formatting problems in Step 5 – so it is better to do it my way right now!)

Now let's go on to our **FPE**. An **FPE** has five paragraphs:

An introductory paragraph

Three paragraphs in the middle – one for each topic

A concluding paragraph

Of course, there are other types of writing we can do: term papers, research papers, book reports, short stories – to name just a few. For the first three, in fact, we do exactly what we have done so far – we just expand our work a bit more. But we don't have to worry about those types of writing right now. (For more information on them, see Postscript 1 on page 41.)

Let's just start working on Step 4.

First, copy our thesis from Step 2. Don't forget to indent this, because we are starting a paragraph.

My writing professor is a self-proclaimed graphophile who loves to help other people become graphophiles like she is.

OK, now what? Well, add Roman Numerals I, II, and III from our outline.

> My writing professor is a self-proclaimed graphophile who loves to help other people become graphophiles like she is. She is very knowledgeable about how a student can improve his or her writing. She puts a great deal of energy into teaching each class. She is one of the most helpful professors I have ever encountered in college.

It's not hard, is it? But we're not finished with the first paragraph; we have to craft it before we go on.

First of all, who is this professor? What is her name? Do we have to say anything more about her before we go into the body of the essay? Yes, we need more. What about this?

> Elizabeth Honaker, my writing professor, is a self-proclaimed graphophile ("one who loves to write") who enjoys teaching other people to become graphophiles like she is. Mizz Liz – as she likes to be called – is very knowledgeable about how a student can improve his or her writing. She puts a great deal of energy into teaching each class. She is one of the most helpful professors I have ever encountered in college.

You will see that I have started to craft my paragraph. Did you notice I included a quick definition of graphophile in the opening sentence? I also included the fact about my nickname in the second sentence. It's relevant at this point, because it hints at the topics and supporting details to follow. But here's an important warning about the introductory paragraph: **Do *not* include too many facts in the first paragraph!!** It happens all the time: Students cram all sorts of facts into their opening paragraph, hoping to impress their reader (the teacher). But it is distracting, and it is the mark of a rambling writer who goes "all over the place" and doesn't bother to organize his or her thoughts. And you don't want to become one of those types of writers, do you?

Are we ready now to go on to the next paragraph?

Not quite! The sentences after the thesis sound a bit too choppy. Let's craft it by combining two of the sentences:

> Elizabeth Honaker, my writing professor, is a self-proclaimed graphophile ("one who loves to write") who enjoys teaching other people to become graphophiles like she is. Mizz Liz – as she likes to be called – is very knowledgeable about how a student can improve his or her writing, and she puts a great deal of energy into teaching each class. She is one of the most helpful professors I have ever encountered in college.

We have to think of a **transition sentence** – something to link the first paragraph with the next paragraph (and we'll be doing this a lot from now on).

So let me help you. Let me suggest how we can form a good transition sentence for this introductory paragraph:

> Elizabeth Honaker, my writing professor, is a self-proclaimed graphophile ("one who loves to write") who enjoys teaching other people to become graphophiles like she is. Mizz Liz – as she likes to be called – is very knowledgeable about how a student can improve his or her writing, and she puts a great deal of energy into teaching each class. <u>With her various methods of challenging her students,</u> she is one of the most helpful professors I have ever encountered in college.

Remember: Nothing is "written in stone" until the minute you hand in your assignment or turn your paper over to your reader. Writing is a continual process of reading and thinking and changing and improving your words and paragraphs and essays. (You would not know this unless I tell you, but I have revised this step – and all the other steps and postscripts in this book – many, many times. I want to get it <u>*exactly*</u> right for you!)

Well, I'm pretty satisfied with our introductory paragraph; I hope you are, too. So let's go on.

Our 2nd paragraph is also pretty much written. We take our topic sentence from Roman Numeral I and combine it with the supporting details to start forming the next paragraph:

> She is very knowledgeable about how a student can improve his or her writing and become a graphophile. Mizz Liz gives lectures which clearly explain each step in writing. She also gives meaningful assignments which demonstrate how to use each of the "five steps to good writing." When she grades assignments, she gives important information about where corrections can be made.

Now, of course you know who "she" is, but it's not good writing style to use a pronoun at the beginning of a paragraph (unless you run out of options). So let's craft the paragraph to read:

> Mizz Liz's ~~is very~~ knowledge~~able~~ about how a student can ~~improve his or her writing and~~ become a graphophile shows in **her clear, step-by-step** lectures ~~which clearly explain each step in writing~~. She also gives meaningful assignments which demonstrate how to use each of the five steps. When she grades assignments, she gives important information about where corrections can be made. **She doesn't want a student to have to guess about how to improve his or her writing.**

Did you notice what I just did? I added and subtracted words (shades of mathematics!!!). The words I added to this paragraph are in green, and the words I subtracted from this paragraph are crossed out in red.

Also notice that I added a transition sentence at the end, and that I used the phrase "improve his or her writing" in this sentence. So I actually moved some things around.

Are you getting the picture?

Now let's do the third paragraph.

> **The fact that this professor** puts a great deal of energy into teaching her ~~class~~ **students shows in every class**. She takes the time to prepare handouts that supplement her lectures. She constantly walks through the class during "seminar time," assisting the students in whatever ways she can, interacting with them like a coach would interact with a sports team. **But that is not all she does.**

Can you identify what I have done to improve this paragraph?

❖ The first thing I did was to change the topic sentence from a simple sentence into a complex sentence.
❖ Instead of "she" as the subject of the sentence, I now have "fact."
❖ Instead of "puts" as the verb, I made "shows" the verb.
❖ Then I changed the word "class" to "students," so that I would not be using the word "class" twice.

Wow! And that was just the FIRST sentence!!

But I did more. I combined my third and fourth sentences into one sentence, linking the idea of having a class seminar with the coach-player relationship on a sports team. So I've given my reader a positive image that might stick better in his or her mind.

My transition sentence is a bit unusual. I teased my reader to go further in my composition. When I wrote, "But that is not all she does," I was in effect saying, "Wait! There's more!"

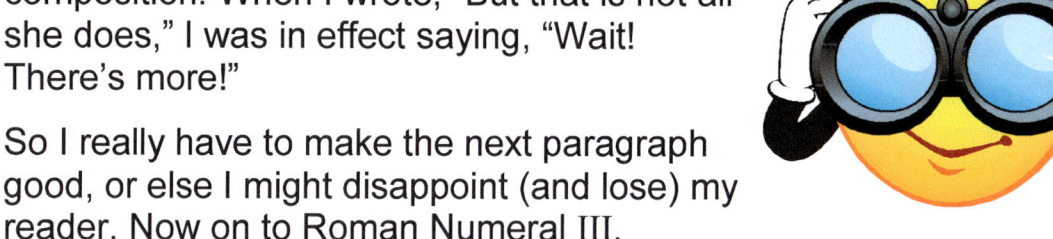

So I really have to make the next paragraph good, or else I might disappoint (and lose) my reader. Now on to Roman Numeral III.

> **Professor Honaker is one of the most helpful professors I have ever encountered in college.** She goes out of her way to encourage frightened or depressed students; **I know, because I was one of them.** She is not afraid to tell you that your writing needs improvement, but she never does it to ~~put you down~~ embarrass or belittle you. **In fact, although she insists on respectful classroom behavior, she is more than willing to forgive misdemeanors, as long as there is positive change on the part of an offending student.**

And there we have it: A third paragraph that speaks to the heart of the reader. As the author, I have tried to relate to each person who is reading the composition. (In other words, does my reader feel scared about writing as the student did? Has he or she been disrespectful or a know-it-all in previous classes? Well, Mizz Liz can handle these types of problems - and more!)

Do you see how we have attempted to save the best idea for last? It is not always possible, but you should try.

Do you also see that I have inserted a personal note into this composition by telling the reader about how this imaginary student was helped by the professor? Many teachers will tell you that it is forbidden to use "I" or "me" anywhere in your essay, and sometimes I agree with them. But sometimes I don't. If used sparingly (like chocolate sauce on a sundae), this type of personal reflection really can fit into your essay or term paper or what-have-you. I especially allow it towards the end of an essay that is a reflection, as this is. (Don't worry about the category of this type of essay. You will find more information on categories in Postscript 1.)

Another thing I did in this paragraph was to ==eliminate slang==. "Put you down" may be perfectly fine in a conversation at a restaurant or on the playing field of your sports team, but in writing compositions for school and college, we want to work towards using better and more descriptive words.

And then I crafted an entirely fresh sentence for the last sentence of my paragraph. It didn't occur to me (as a writer) to include this in my outline, but it is good to include more ideas into your paragraphs as you go along, as long as you don't go off on a tangent.

What's a tangent? Think of it as a rabbit hole that you suddenly discover as you are walking down the path you have chosen. You're eager to find out what the resident rabbit looks like! So you go exploring, and you go off your chosen path. It may be fun to find the rabbit, but it's not fun for your reader to be taken down the hole with you!

So don't do it.

Are you excited yet? We are about to work on our last paragraph – our conclusion! But now we have to be careful.

If you will think back, we haven't included any information about this paragraph into our outline. Although some writing teachers don't agree with me, I have a very good reason for not including a section for the conclusion in our outline (Step 3).

During **Step 4**, we have been crafting our writing – changing it to flow better, to read better, etc. When we change one thing, we often have to change another thing and another thing and another thing – these things have a "knock-on" effect.

Let's say that we did a lot of changing to paragraphs 2, 3, and 4. If we had already planned out the conclusion in detail and then written the conclusion without considering our changes, we might make our readers scratch their heads and say, "Huh? I don't get it." So I say: Wait and write the conclusion after you're happy about the first four paragraphs of your essay.

Oh...that's right...we haven't talked about what a conclusion really does for your composition. Let's do that now.

One thing it does is that it ties everything you've said into a neat package, like a birthday present: The ends of the wrapping paper are taped neatly, the bow won't fall off, and you've remembered to write who the present is for.

There are three purposes for a conclusion: summary, reflection, and application. These are big words, but they're worth exploring, so here goes:

Summary is like the tape on the wrapping around the birthday present. To summarize something, you take all the ends and relate them ("tape them") back to the thesis.

Reflection is like the bow on your present. You make the present prettier with the bow, and you show you've carefully thought about how to give this gift to your friend on her birthday. To reflect is to give something of your own thought or opinion about the thesis. (Don't make it mushy or sentimental, though!)

Application is like the gift card on the present. It shows the reader how the composition applies to him or to her. Although your friend will guess that the present you hold in your hand is for her – especially if you show up at her door, there's a birthday party going on, and you actually hand the present to *her* – it's always nice to say, "Here. This is for you."

So how would this look if we wrote a conclusion for this composition on your crazy professor?

Well, here's my two-cents-worth:

> Writing professors come in all shapes and sizes. Professor Honaker is not the only good writing instructor out there. But she is unique, and people like me who have experienced her in class know this to be a fact. Good writing is essential to college studies, and graphophiles like Mizz Liz help to ensure good writing continues to be taught.

Notice the following:

- **Summary**: I don't spend time concentrating on what a graphophile is. I used the word to launch into a description of what a good writing instructor does, so I use it once again to "tape the wrapping paper" together.

- **Reflection**: The phrase "people like me" shows the reader how the professor has impacted at least one person's life.

❖ **Application**: "Good writing is essential to college studies" takes the composition out into the world of the reader.

Now it's time to pause and let the whole composition sit for a little while. (This is why procrastination is not good for writing! You have to have <u>time</u> between Steps 4 & 5.)

Go get some comfort food. Go ride a bike, or do your chores or play a video game (yes, you can do that – but not for TOO long!). Then come back for Step 5.

Step 5: Revision

This is the step that all sorts of students think they can skip. "I've gotten my composition done. Why do I have to do more?"

You have to do more because – deep down – you know the difference between being a conscientious student and being a hack (not a hack**_er_**).

Conscientious Student =

You want to learn and improve

Hack =

You don't really care about learning; you just want to finish the course.

I want you to become a CS!!

Revision looks at the whole composition and searches for ways to improve it.

Some improvements that can be made:

- Grammar
- Punctuation
- Spelling
- Facts
- Sentence structure
- Flow of thoughts
- Presentation

Now I will tell you a little secret – actually, it's no secret. I tell my students about it all the time. Here it is:

I'm not perfect and I make mistakes, even in my writing.

And if I make mistakes, I <u>want</u> to correct them. The difference between me and some of my students, however, is that some of my students are satisfied as long as the composition "looks finished" (whatever that means):

- Maybe the paper has been neatly typed (always good).
- Maybe the student has put the correct heading on the paper (good idea).
- Maybe the student has the correct number of paragraphs or the correct number of pages (that helps).
- Maybe the student thinks that working on a composition for an hour or two is "good enough."

Nope. N–O...NO!

When someone thinks something is "good enough," that's a sure sign that the student has cut corners and hasn't given the paper his or her full attention.

And there's another problem in the land of "good enough." Everything you write (except maybe your diary) – all your papers, all your tests, all your postings on social media – will be seen (now or later) by someone else. And that person will probably be someone who wants or needs to form an opinion about your writing skill:

- ❖ **A teacher**
- ❖ **A professor**
- ❖ **Your parents**
- ❖ **Your friends**
- ❖ **Strangers**
- ❖ **Employers**
- ❖ **Your grandchildren** (yep, them, too!)

So I encourage you to think ahead and decide to be that CS I've been talking about.

Back to revision. Here's where all your writing exercises and grammar assignments and spelling lists and language studies all work together to help you <mark>communicate</mark> your ideas to your readers. (Did you understand you wanted to communicate? Well, now you do!)

You will not always know if you have made a mistake, especially if you are a young writer just starting out. That is why you need to learn the rules and nuances of the English language. Don't be afraid of using dictionaries and thesauri. Don't think that grammar guides are for wimps.

We have finished our five steps, but there is just a bit more to discuss before we close the book.

Postscript 1: Types of Compositions

Book Reports – These papers tell what happens in a book. They do not give any interpretation of what goes on there.

Essays – These compositions have at least five paragraphs. They attempt to interpret ideas from literature, or the actions of characters, etc. Here are some of the most common ones:

Narrative: You tell a story in order to make a point. This is not a creative writing exercise, though. The story has to have happened to you or to someone you know.

Descriptive: You describe a setting or place in order to set a certain mood for your reader.

Expository: You explain an idea or a process.

Persuasive: You try to get your reader to accept your opinion about something, and you provide as much proof as you can.

Compare and Contrast: You take two ideas, characters, etc., and you explain to your reader the things that are similar and the things that are different between the two.

Analytical: You explain the deeper meanings in a theme or concept.

Argumentative: You argue strongly for a particular point of view. However, you never write in a nasty or rude way. Here is where the principles of logic are *very* useful.

Term Papers – These are expanded essays. Each topic for your thesis will have at least two paragraphs; the paper will be at least three pages long.

Research Papers – These are written after you have researched a topic in at least two outside sources (like books, newspapers, magazines, internet websites, etc.). They are usually longer than term papers.

Postscript 2: A Few Suggested Exercises

For free writing:

- Think up 8 bullets about someone you know.
- Think up 8 bullets about your pet.
- Think up 8 bullets about your favorite hobby.
- Think up 10 bullets about fixing something mechanical.
- Think up 10 bullets about your favorite book.
- Think up 12 bullets on something you are eager to research.

For writing a thesis:

- Write a thesis arguing that potato chips (or some other comfort food you like) are good for you (don't use the word "good").
- Write a thesis trying to persuade your friend that it is a good thing to do chores (again, don't use the word "good").
- Write a thesis showing how much you liked the last book you read (don't use the word "like" or "love").
- Write a thesis comparing a book to its movie (be sure to include the name of the book, its author, and the name of the movie).
- Write a thesis for the subject you decided to research in the previous group of assignments.

For an outline:

- Pick one thesis from the above exercises in "For writing a thesis" and write an outline with 3 topics.
- Pretend you have written a thesis about your cat's silly behavior; then write an outline with three topics.
- From either one of the above assignments, support one topic with three examples (the "A," "B," and "C").
- Write an outline telling your reader three ways in which you appreciate your parents.
- Write an outline based on the following thesis: "The United States is a country worth defending."

For a composition:

- ❖ Pick one of the first two exercises in "For an outline" and write an introductory paragraph which includes the thesis and the topics. Don't forget to craft a transition sentence.
- ❖ Write two paragraphs for one of your topics in your "appreciating your parents" outline.
- ❖ Write a paragraph on one of your topics in "the U.S. is worth defending" assignment.
- ❖ Write a paragraph on the subject you researched under "free writing."

Postscript 3: Vocabulary and Other Language Tools

"The difference between the right word and the almost-right word is the difference between lightning and a lightning bug."

~~ Mark Twain

Choosing the right word when you are writing is essential for good **communication**. Many people are sloppy when it comes to choosing their words, and then they wonder why their reader does not understand them – or even dislikes reading what they write!

Say, for instance, that you wanted to talk about your cat. You wouldn't use the words "dog" or "parakeet" in your speech or your composition to represent "cat," would you? Your reader would be confused with your vocabulary. You would want to use the right word so you can communicate.

Now let's suppose we talk about patriotism. It's a little harder to do because "patriotism" is an abstract noun, not a concrete noun like "cat."

"**Patriotism**" does not walk in through the door or rub against your hand or sit and "meow" at you. It is an **idea** in our heads and is more difficult to describe. So we need to use **vocabulary** in a different way.

45

How do we get a better vocabulary?
How do we know which word to use – and when to use it?

It is here where dictionaries and other types of language tools come in quite handy. You wouldn't try to build a soapbox racer with only a hammer, would you? You wouldn't try to paint a picture with just water and a brush or two, would you? These are activities that require you to build skills with certain kinds of **tools** and materials. So please read what I'm going to say about **language tools**.

A **dictionary** is an alphabetical listing of words and their definitions. It also has other information, like the history of the word, when it was first used in the English language, and so on. Remember all the pieces of wood that you saw in that house frame on page 11? Each word in a composition is like a piece of wood in that house. A word communicates an idea – something that has meaning in the language you are using – and is a very valuable tool. So using it correctly is pretty important.

A **thesaurus** is another great language tool. It is a book that gives you synonyms (words with similar meanings) and antonyms (words with opposite meanings) for a particular word. With a little practice, it is as easy to use as a dictionary.

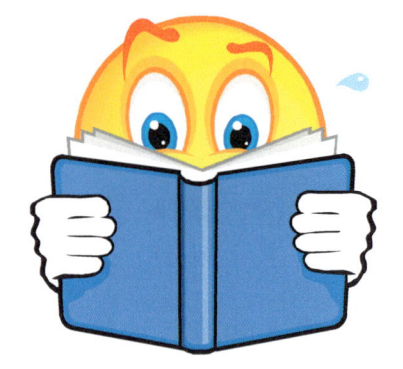

A **spelling book** and a **grammar book** are also very useful, but many students think that spelling and grammar rules are boring and unnecessary, until they get to sentences like these:

Lettuce eat Grandma.

The horse raced past the barn fell.

What can we make of these sentences? Are they bad writing or bad something-else?

"Lettuce" might be an incorrect word choice (or even a misspelling). What if we substituted "let us"? Then the first sentence would read:

Let us eat Grandma. (?)

Well, we're a little closer to some kind of meaning that makes sense – except that my _own_ grandmother was a bit of a "tough old bird" – as the British say – and definitely would _not_ appreciate being eaten!

So let's think... I know!

What if we are talking _to_ Grandma instead of contemplating whether or not to make *her* Sunday _dinner_? Then the sentence would read:

Let's eat, Grandma!

And now we have discovered the real meaning of the sentence: Grandma is a _wonderful_ cook, and we can't _wait_ to eat the meal she has prepared!

Do you see how spelling and punctuation help us to communicate better?

See what meaning we can get out of the second sentence by using some punctuation.

The horse ran, past the barn, fell.

Does this really make sense? We perceive the horse ran, but there is an awkward pause between "barn" and "fell" – a comma always indicates a pause – and we are unsure what has happened "past the barn."

The horse ran past; the barn fell.

With this punctuation, we have both nouns ("horse" and "barn") connected to verbs ("ran" and "fell"). The semicolon suggests a connection between the two events, and that finally makes sense.

These are only two examples of the practical use of spelling and grammar studies. There are many, many more.

Here are more suggestions to improve vocabulary skills:

1. One way is to **read** and to **think** about what you are reading. That way your brain stores away good words to use, especially if the composition is well-written. So read good books, magazines, and articles constantly!

2. Another way is to use books that teach you words that you would not ordinarily encounter. Books that reveal the Latin and Greek roots of English words are not hard to use once you start.

3. *A third way is to participate in class discussions. Some of your classmates or friends may use words that are unfamiliar to you, but this should not annoy you (unless they are being rude or insulting). In fact, a good CS will learn new vocabulary all the time — in class, at home, at the grocery store, in the movies, etc.*

(Remember what a CS is? Check back to page 37 if you don't.)

A fourth way is to write and keep writing. Then show your writing to other people and see if they understand exactly what you are saying. Ask them if they see any misspelled words or grammatical mistakes. Do not be angry if you receive correction; it is part of the process of becoming a good writer.

IV

A fifth way is to take notes in class or while reading. Many students have complained to me that they don't appreciate "old-fashioned" ideas like note-taking and writing practice. And I say to them: "Old-fashioned" is a phrase that has no meaning in my classroom. If a technique _works_ – and I wouldn't suggest it unless it _does_ work – then it doesn't matter if Methuselah once used it!

But something even older than Methuselah is at work here. Our brains work in marvelous ways, and scientists are now able to tell us:

1. People who write down what they hear are (consciously or unconsciously) making significant judgments that help with the learning process.
2. Recording information through more than one sense (in this case, one's sense of sight and one's sense of touch) helps the information to "stick."
3. Writing (or typing) information down in note form makes it easier to review and remember later.

True ✓ False ☐

Old or new, easy or hard – these labels are irrelevant if they help us to accomplish our goal to write and communicate better. Isn't that true?

49

Postscript 4: Word Processors

I am not a computer genius, and I don't really understand how computers work. But I have picked up a few things from my computer genius husband.

If you are going to use a computer to write, you have to have software (operating instructions) for the computer to take what you type and to turn it into a document (eventually a paper).

These are called **word processors**.

There are several software programs that work well on computers, but almost all of them cost money – all except for OpenOffice, which you download through the internet and which is completely free. It works well as a word processor. You or your parents might want to consider using this program. The website address is:

https://www.openoffice.org/

I wish you luck in your writing journey.
Don't forget to let me know how you are
doing!

Sincerely,

Mizz Liz

Made in the USA
Charleston, SC
10 September 2014